CONTENTS

ALL THE FUN OF THE FAIR!

Fairgrounds are places for thrills and scares on daredevil rides. Over the years, rides have become more and more terrifying as designers and engineers seek to create the ultimate experience for thrill seekers.

HOW DID FAIRS BEGIN?

Fairs started when people got together to buy and sell, find work or celebrate festivals. One of the earliest was the Stagshaw Bank Fair in Northumberland, UK, which started as a gathering for selling animals around 1293. By the 1850s fairs had games, spectacles and rides to entertain the crowds.

Carousels and rides have been part of St Giles Fair in Oxford, UK, for over 150 years.

RIDES of the WORLD

Wooden rollercoaster
The fastest wooden rollercoaster with the largest drop of 55 m is Goliath at Six Flags Great America, Illinois, USA, built in 2004.

4th dimension rollercoaster
The first 4th dimension rollercoaster was X2, built in 2002 at Six Flags Magic Mountain, Santa Clarita, California, USA.

Carousel
The world's largest indoor carousel is at House on the Rock in Spring Green, Wisconsin, USA. It has 269 carousel animals and 20,000 lights.

The oldest carousel is in Wilhelmsbad Park, Hanau, Germany. It is more like a roundabout than a galloper. It dates from 1780.

Bumper cars
One of the most unusual bumper-car tracks has to be on board the cruise ship Quantum of the Seas.

4

FAIR POWER

Basic rides like swingboats, 'over the top' wheels, and roundabouts developed over time into the exciting rides we know today. Early rides were powered by hand, sometimes by children in return for a free go! Larger rides, like roundabouts, were horse powered.

From the 1860s, steam power took over and traction engines were used to move the rides. Later, these amazing machines were replaced by electricity.

Fairgrounds have adapted existing machines that used basic engineering like wheels, cogs and chains. Many rides share the same principles of forces and motion, but change the experience by adding extra speed, height, turns or total darkness for even bigger shocks and scares. So, take your seats, hold on tight and enjoy the ride!

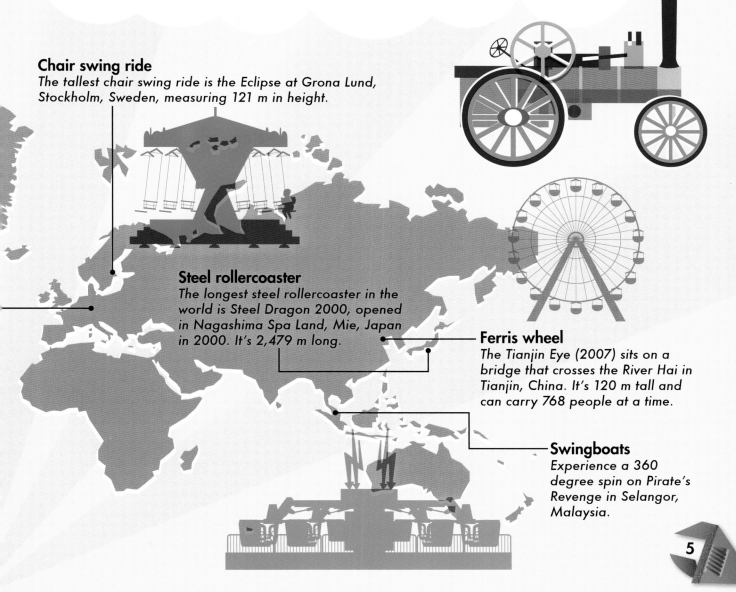

Chair swing ride
The tallest chair swing ride is the Eclipse at Grona Lund, Stockholm, Sweden, measuring 121 m in height.

Steel rollercoaster
The longest steel rollercoaster in the world is Steel Dragon 2000, opened in Nagashima Spa Land, Mie, Japan in 2000. It's 2,479 m long.

Ferris wheel
The Tianjin Eye (2007) sits on a bridge that crosses the River Hai in Tianjin, China. It's 120 m tall and can carry 768 people at a time.

Swingboats
Experience a 360 degree spin on Pirate's Revenge in Selangor, Malaysia.

SWINGBOATS

One of the very first rides to become popular at travelling fairs was the swingboat. Its backwards and forwards swinging motion formed the basis of future fairground attractions, known as pendulum rides.

Build a hand-powered ride based on a swinging motion.

Inventor: Swingboats have been around since the early 1800s; the inventor is unknown.

Key location: The Skylark at Beamish Open-Air Museum, UK is one of the oldest swingboats in the world. It dates back to the 1830s.

Axle attached to the top of the A-frame

Rope

Rope

Boat, also called a gondola

Swingboats in action

PULLING POWER

Swingboats need muscle power to get them started. Riders, one at each end of the boat, pull on hanging ropes to make the boat swing. As one rider pulls down on their rope, the nose of the boat rises. As it swings back in an arc, the opposite rider pulls on their rope, and the swingboat goes higher in the opposite direction.

NEWTON'S FIRST LAW OF MOTION

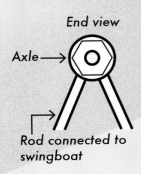
End view
Axle →
Rod connected to swingboat

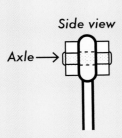
Side view
Axle →

The constant swinging motion is an example of Newton's first law of motion, which says that an object that is still will stay still unless it is moved, and an object that is moving will stay moving unless something stops it.

When the riders stop pulling on the ropes, friction starts to slow the boat down. Friction occurs as the surfaces of the axle and the rods rub against each other, as well as in the form of air resistance, as the boat pushes through the air. Eventually friction brings the boat to a halt.

GIANT PENDULUM

A swingboat acts like a giant pendulum, swinging in a fixed path under its own weight. It needs power to make it move upwards for the first swing, then gravity pulls the boat down, and a force called inertia keeps it moving, pushing the swingboat back into the air. This process works again and again to make the boat swing back and forth. The riders can keep pulling on the ropes to pull the boat into the air and maintain the momentum of this swinging sensation!

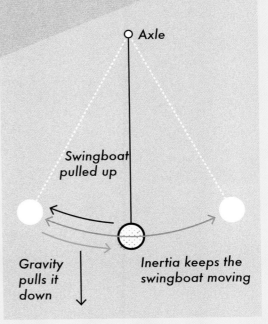
○ Axle
Swingboat pulled up
Gravity pulls it down
Inertia keeps the swingboat moving

MAUCH CHUNK SWITCHBACK RAILWAY

The Mauch Chunk Switchback Railway in Pennsylvania was the first rollercoaster in the USA. It wasn't designed to be a fun ride; when it was built in 1827, it was designed to transport coal.

BECOMING A RIDE

The railway began taking passengers in 1829. The uphill journey was powered by mules pulling the carriage along a single-track railroad. This took four hours, whereas gravity powered the speedy half-hour ride downhill. Passengers found the journey thrilling and flocked to ride on it. From 1872 it was run entirely for fun, and carried over 35,000 passengers a year.

BUILDING BRIEF

Build a railroad to move coal between Mauch Chunk and Summit Hill.

Engineer: Josiah White

Location: Pennsylvania, USA

Rails work by guiding the train or carriage over a set route. The rails provide a low-friction track, which transfers some of the weight of the train to the ground through the sleepers and loose ballast surround. The rails are fixed to the sleepers, but are not fixed to the ballast, so as the train moves over the rails its weight is transferred to the ground.

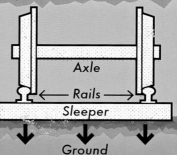

Axle

Rails

Sleeper

Loose ballast →

Ground

ANTI-ROLLBACK DEVICE

In 1846, the mules were retired and the carriages were pulled uphill by a winch and cable. A new ratchet safety feature was also fitted to the underside of the carriages. This was the first kind of anti-rollback device. A device called a pawl hangs from the underside of the car and catches on a ratchet strip on the track. This simple mechanism stops the cars from rolling downhill if the cable breaks. The ratchet and pawl make a loud, rickety clatter as they knock together. The device is still used on rollercoasters today and enthusiasts love the tension this builds on the steep uphill climbs.

Pawl →

Ratchet

The Switchback Railway at Coney Island opened in 1884. It was the first American rollercoaster built as a ride and featured two parallel wavy tracks. Riders travelled sideways, sitting on a seat a little like a park bench. They sped along one track to the end, got off and the park bench and riders were 'switched' onto the other track to whoosh back to the beginning.

CAROUSEL

The carousel, also known as a merry-go-round or flying horses, is an iconic fairground ride. The first carousel was a simple wooden roundabout, which in the 1700s was powered by horses or people, but it was the adoption of steam power in the mid-1800s that really got this ride galloping!

BUILDING BRIEF

Create a carousel that is not powered by horses or people, and add a galloping motion.

Inventors: Thomas Bradshaw's steam-powered carousel appeared in 1861; Frederick Savage invented the galloping mechanism in 1870.

Location: Norfolk, UK

Around 63 kg of coal was needed to power the carousel steam engine for one day of rides.

STEAM GALLOPERS

In 1861 Thomas Bradshaw built the first set of steam-powered carousel horses; he called this ride 'gallopers'. The steam engine turns a drive shaft that has a cog at the end of it. This cog turns an angled bevel gear that is fixed to an upright pole. This in turn moves a ring gear in the canopy and the carousel spins round.

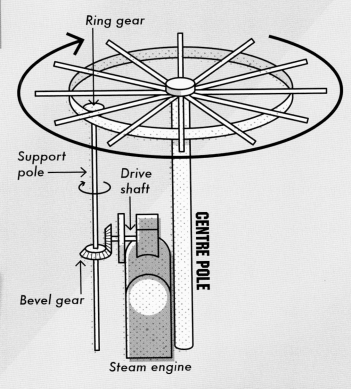

Ring gear

Support pole

Drive shaft

CENTRE POLE

Bevel gear

Steam engine

Steam-driven gallopers in London, 1903

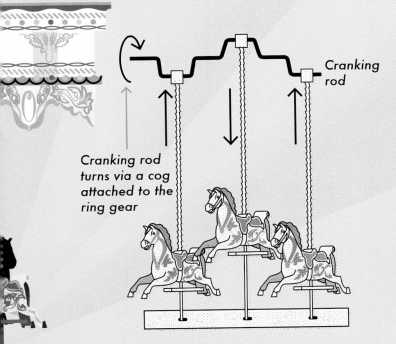

Cranking rod

Cranking rod turns via a cog attached to the ring gear

GEARS AND CRANKS

Later in 1870, Frederick Savage added a gear and offset crank mechanism to his steam-powered horses, making them rise and fall at different times during the ride. Each horse is connected via a pole to a cranking rod in the canopy. The cranking rod is not straight, but wiggly, so each horse connected along the rod hangs at a different height.

As the ride revolves, so does the cranking rod, causing the horses to be lifted and lowered at different times – as if they are galloping. The pole that the horse is attached to goes through a hole in the floor platform. This hole allows the poles to move a little way outwards as the ride goes faster.

CHAIR SWING RIDE

Chair swing rides, also known as Chair-O-Planes or wave swingers, developed from carousels. One of the first steam-driven rides was built by John Inshaw in 1888. Here, the seat is not restrained at the bottom and the passenger is lifted into the air on a swing seat, flying outwards as the central column of the ride spins faster and faster.

BUILDING BRIEF

Use the spinning steam-driven technology of the carousel to create a new wilder ride.

Inventor: John Inshaw

Key locations:
Chair-O-Plane (1888), Birmingham, UK

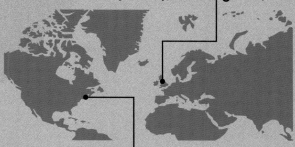

SkyScreamer (2011),
Six Flags, New Jersey, USA

FORCES

The central frame of the swing ride rotates at speed, with the hanging seats reacting to the spinning force, flying out to the sides. This movement is caused by the balancing of two opposing forces, centrifugal and centripetal force.

CENTRIFUGAL FORCE pushes outwards, moving the seats away from the centre of the ride.

CENTRIPETAL FORCE pushes the seats back in towards the centre. The opposition of these forces creates tension in the chairs' chains making the chairs rise to an almost horizontal level and giving the riders an amazing flying sensation.

Centrifugal force

Centripetal force

Centre of the ride

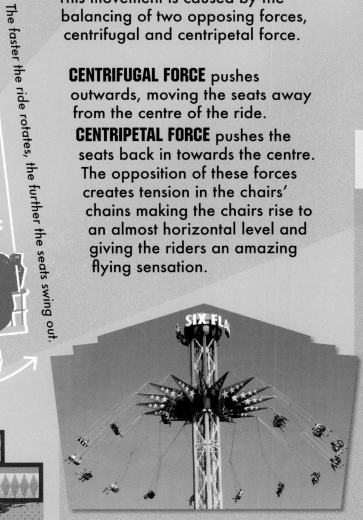

The faster the ride rotates, the further the seats swing out.

SKYSCREAMER

In 2011, an extreme version of this ride, the SkyScreamer (pictured), was opened in Six Flags, New England, USA. It is the tallest chair swing ride in the world and lifts the riders over 122 m into the air, and rotates them at 64 km/h. The tower is made up of six upright struts, joined together by a pattern of diagonal supports. The crisscrossed design makes it strong, and allows the wind at the top to whistle through the structure, and not make it sway and bend out of shape.

FERRIS WHEEL

The first Ferris wheel was built as a giant engineering spectacle for visitors to the World's Columbian Exposition in Chicago, Illinois, USA in 1893. The upright 80-m-tall wheel had room for 2,160 passengers at a time!

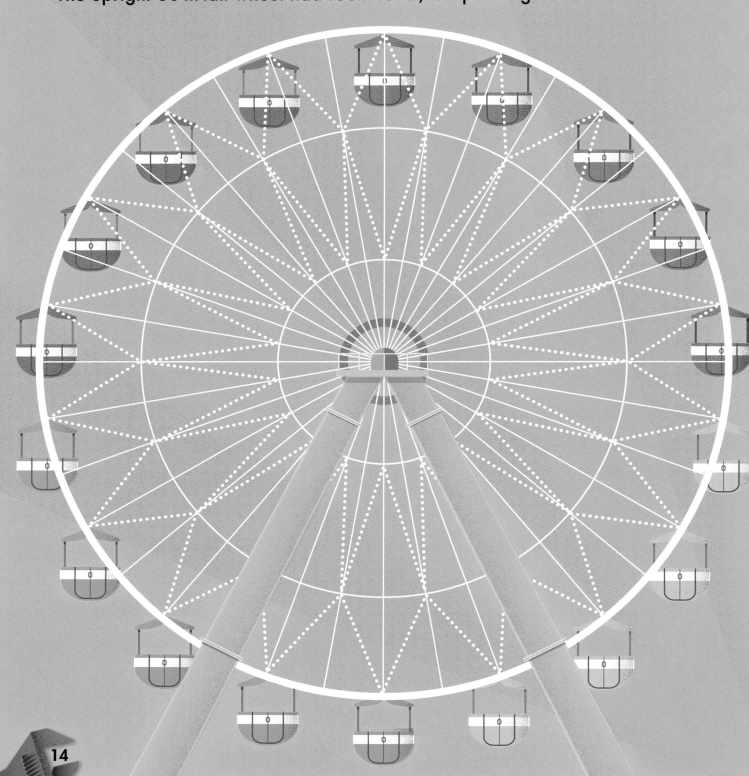

BUILDING BRIEF

Design a ride built in steel that will astound and delight visitors to the Columbian Exposition, held to celebrate the 400th anniversary of Columbus landing in America.

Inventor: George Washington Gale Ferris Jr.

Key location: Chicago, USA

UPWARDS AND DOWNWARDS

Ferris's super strong steel structure consisted of a large wheel rotating on a central axis held by two towers. The ride upwards was powered by a steam engine driving the turns with the help of gears, like a giant carousel turned on its side. The ride downwards is helped by the pull of gravity, kept under control by the gear mechanism.

The passenger cars hang off axles at the edge of the wheel and they swing as the ride moves, but gravity keeps them hanging downwards and the riders safely in their seats.

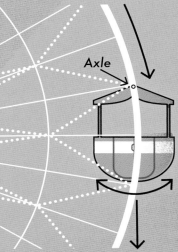

Direction of rotation

Axle

Pull of gravity

THE POWER OF THE TRIANGLE

The Ferris wheel is held in place by a large steel triangular frame and the spokes of the wheel fan outward in triangular shapes. Ferris knew through designing and building bridges that long spans of wood or metal could be strengthened by adding crisscrossed supports making triangle shapes. The triangle is the strongest shape to use. Because forces move evenly throughout the three sides and corners, it is more successful at resisting stress than other shapes.

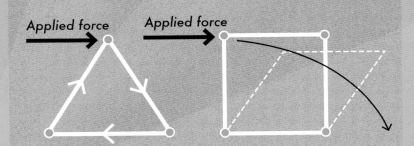

Applied force *Applied force*

When the wheel was unveiled, George W Ferris said he had got the wheels out of his head and made them a living reality.

BUMPER CARS

Electric bumper cars are one of the most popular fairground rides of them all. Also known as dodgems, these small round cars with their big, rubber bumpers allow anyone – no matter how old or young – to drive, bump and bash into each other.

BUILDING BRIEF

Build a ride that is controlled by the rider – a car that can be driven, raced and bumped all around the track.

Inventors: Victor Levand of New York City invented them, but Max and Harold Stoehrer of Massachusetts registered the idea.

Key location: New York City and Massachusetts, USA

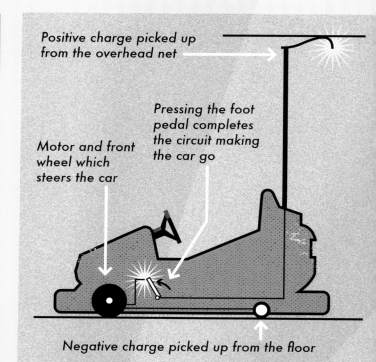

Positive charge picked up from the overhead net →

Pressing the foot pedal completes the circuit making the car go

Motor and front wheel which steers the car

Negative charge picked up from the floor

BUMPER CAR CIRCUIT

One of the major innovations that changed fairground rides was the introduction of electricity. The first bumper cars worked by completing a simple electrical circuit. The power supply ran through an overhead net and travelled down to the car through a metal pole. The cars had three wheels – two rubber ones at the back and a metal wheel to conduct electricity at the front. The track surface was also conductive. When the bumper car pedal was pressed, the circuit was complete; the motor rotated the wheels via a belt and the car jumped into action.

BUMPING MOTION

When the bumper cars bump into each other, we have a perfect example of Newton's third law of motion. This states that for every action, there is an equal and opposite reaction.

As the cars collide, the force with which they were moving and the mass they contain gets distributed around the rubber bumper, but also makes the riders jolt, as the energy transfers between the cars. Each collision is different because of the speed and direction the cars travel and the weight of the riders.

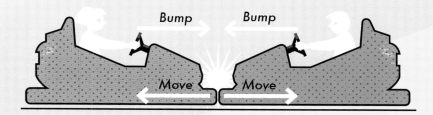

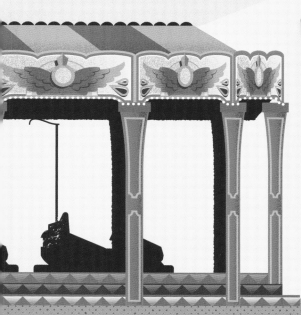

Modern dodgems are powered by metal strips on the floor, connecting to brushes under the car.

BIG DIPPER

People love to be scared and what better way to be terrified than to hurtle around a rickety wooden track in a tiny car, at great speed? The Big Dipper at Blackpool Pleasure Beach, which opened in 1923, does just this. It was the first rollercoaster to be built in the UK that included a big drop with a complete circuit. The Big Dipper is still standing today.

BUILDING BRIEF

Design a spectacular ride for the British funfair at Blackpool Pleasure Beach.

Inventor: John A Miller, 1923

Location: Blackpool, UK

LIFT-HILL MECHANISM

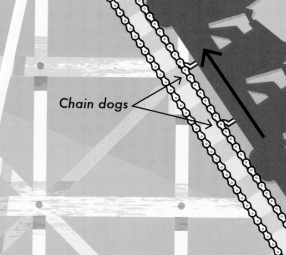

Lift-hill mechanism

Chain dogs

The Big Dipper starts with a long, steep climb followed by a massive drop. The climb is supported by the 'lift-hill' mechanism, invented in 1885, by Phillip Hinkle. This has a looped chain running around two wheels at the top and bottom of the upward track. The chain is exposed to the underside of the car as it moves along the rails. Chain dogs, which are big hooks hanging down from the car, catch onto the chain and this drags the car upwards. At the top of the hill, the chain dog is released, gravity takes over and the car plunges down the track.

The Big Dipper at Blackpool Pleasure Beach, 1930s

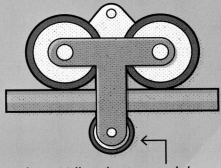

John A Miller also invented the up-lift wheel in 1912. This is a third wheel running under the rails that helps keep the car on the tracks even at the bumpiest moments.

POTENTIAL AND KINETIC ENERGY

The Big Dipper is an 'out and back' design, which means it runs in a complete circuit. After the initial big climb and spectacular fall the rest of the run is tamer, because the car is powered by the potential and kinetic energy produced on that first big opening climb and drop.

As the car goes uphill it gathers potential energy, and at the top of the climb it stops. At this point, because of the height, it has reached the point of maximum potential energy. The potential energy is changed into kinetic energy to power the car for the rest of the ride. The balance of potential and kinetic energy was carefully considered by engineers throughout the Big Dipper ride so the car can complete the run.

Wooden rollercoasters are often built from pine or Douglas fir trees, which grow strong and straight.

● Potential energy

● Maximum potential energy

○ Kinetic energy

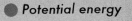

ORBITER

With its use of hydraulics, the Orbiter was a new and innovative ride. It's a fast-paced spinning ride that has become a favourite for fairground thrill seekers since it launched in 1976.

BUILDING BRIEF

Use hydraulics to create a fairground ride that is fast, exciting and totally new!

Inventors: Richard Woolls

Key location: First appeared in Margate, UK

MOVEMENTS

The Orbiter moves in three ways: the cars move round in a circle; the cars move up and down as the main arms rise and fall through a 90 degree angle; the cars at the end of the arm spin. These three movements create a wildly exciting ride pattern. The use of hydraulics make the ride exceptionally quiet, but an explosion of lights and music make up for the lack of mechanical noise.

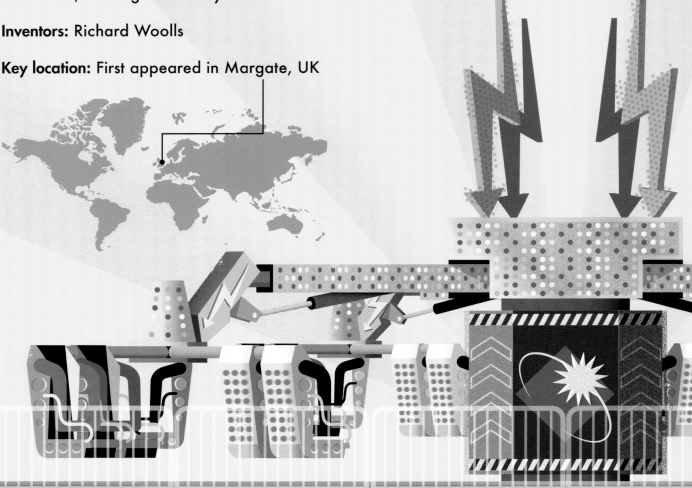

HOW DO HYDRAULICS WORK?

Hydraulics work by placing a force onto one point, which then moves another point. The force is transferred through a liquid that cannot be compressed, in this case oil. The oil presses against the pistons, and the pistons move the arms of the Orbiter.

The hydraulic system has to be closed, with enough power in the engine and enough liquid in the system to move the arms on the Orbiter ride upwards. When the ride is finished an opposite pressure has to be applied to the arm system to make it come back down to earth.

The centre part of the ride lifts off the ground with more hydraulics. Once it has lifted the riders clear of the ground it starts to rotate. The central column rotates at 20 rpm and the arms at 30 rpm, resulting in a fast-moving whirlwind of a ride!

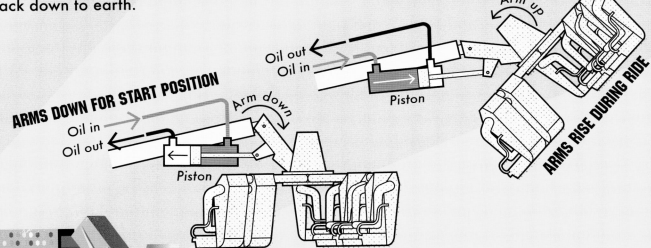

Arm up

Oil out
Oil in

Piston

ARMS RISE DURING RIDE

ARMS DOWN FOR START POSITION

Arm down

Oil in

Oil out

Piston

HYDRAULIC REVOLUTION

Since the Orbiter, hydraulic engineering has become a common feature in fairground rides. They are used in the breaking and launching systems on rollercoasters, and to lower and secure the safety restraints that hold passengers in their seats.

SLINGSHOT

Unveiled in 2004, the Slingshot is like a huge catapult. It has a car holding two passengers connected to twin towers by steel cables. The car is anchored at ground level and when released shoots the car up into the sky. For riders, the sensation is like that of an arrow being fired from a bow. It's like a bungee jump, in reverse!

BUILDING BRIEF

Construct a ride based on the idea of a slingshot, which propels the riders high into the air.

Manufacturer: Funtime, Bundall Australia

Key location: Bundall, Australia

SPRING TIME

Some catapult rides have elastic bungee ropes that fling the passenger carriage into the air, but the Slingshot uses an advanced system of springs and pulleys to power the car. When the seat is secured to the ground, the coiled springs are stretched out. Then, when the slingshot car is released, the springs shoot back into their coiled shape, pinging the car high into the air.

The ride even has a computer that adjusts the force needed to propel the car into the air, whatever the weight of the passengers – clever!

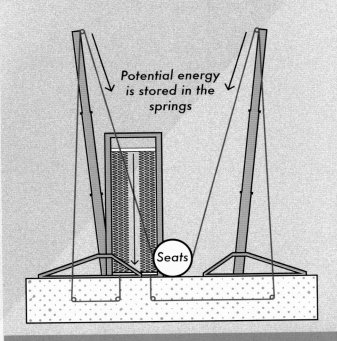

Potential energy is stored in the springs

Seats

The super high towers of the Slingshot are 60 m tall.

ENERGY TRANSFER

Before the ride starts, the tension in the cable is storing potential energy. Once the catapult is released and the car springs upwards, it becomes kinetic energy, the energy of motion. Potential energy is created by the height the car continues to climb to and kinetic energy is released on the downward path.

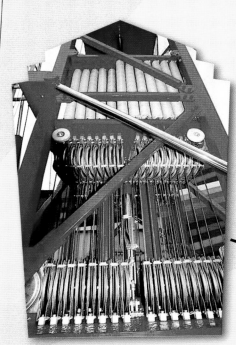

The Slingshot uses 720 springs to fire people up, up, and away!

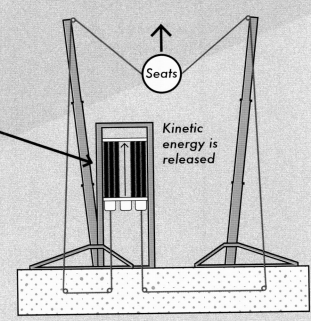

Seats

Kinetic energy is released

KINGDA KA AND ZUMANJARO

If one fairground ride seems a bit dull, how about two rides joined together? Kingda Ka runs along twisting tubular steel tracks that allow it to loop and corkscrew through 360 degrees. Zumanjaro is a drop ride that sits on the curving loop of the Kingda Ka. Together, they add up to two truly terrifying rides.

BUILDING BRIEF

Build a super-fast and tall rollercoaster, then add to the feeling of danger by linking it to a terrifying drop ride.

Designer: Kingda Ka – Werner Stengel; Zumanjaro – Michael Reitz

Manufacturer: Intamin

Map location: Jackson, New Jersey, USA

KINGDA KA

At 139 m, Kingda Ka is the tallest rollercoaster in the world. It's a simple loop-coaster, with lots of corkscrew twists. The car is propelled along the track at great speed by an hydraulic launch system. The car is hooked onto an extended cable, connected to a winch drum powered by hydraulic motors. The motor spins the winch drum, winding in the cable at high speed. This action pulls the cable and attached car along the track and then casts the car off to speed over the gigantic loop.

It takes the car 3.5 seconds to reach 206 km/h and the whole ride is over in 28 seconds. Sometimes the car doesn't quite make it over the top, so it rolls back to the start to try again ... terrifying!

The tubular steel tracks allow for a 360 degree twisting corkscrew turn.

STATION

Cars ⟶

ZUMANJARO

Its official name is Zumanjaro: Drop of Doom. And as the name suggests, this is a drop ride. It winches three horizontal cars holding 24 people up the 126 m frame using a cable. The tension builds as it climbs slowly to the top, halting for a few seconds, then the car plummets down to earth at 145 km/h!

Zumanjaro uses an electromagnetic brake system. These work by having a copper conductor attached to the car, and a magnet field at the bottom of the drop. When the conductor on the car reaches the magnet, it creates its own magnetic field, and when one magnetic field moves over another, they react by producing an opposing force. In this case, it is an upward force at the bottom that slows down the car, stopping the freefall.

FREEFALL SENSATIONS

Both these rides play with your senses as they go into freefall. As the acceleration of the ride pulling you back in your seat is equal to the force of gravity pulling you forward out of your seat, you feel momentarily weightless.

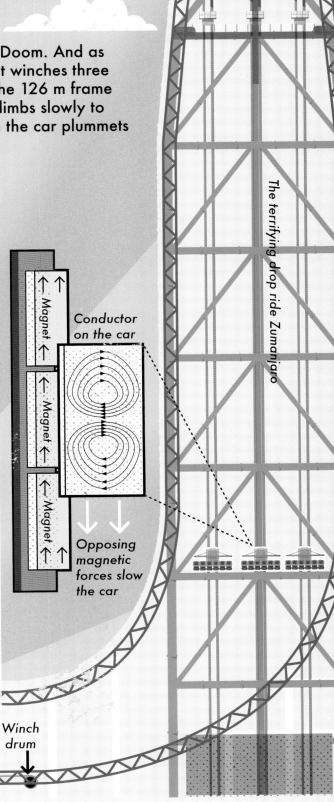

Magnet

Magnet

Magnet

Conductor on the car

Opposing magnetic forces slow the car

The terrifying drop ride Zumanjaro

The giant looping Kingda Ka rollercoaster

Cable

Winch drum

EEJANAIKA

Opened in 2006, Eejanaika is a rollercoaster with a twist. The riders sit in seats that extend either side of the track to give the feeling of hanging in the air. As the car speeds and turns, the riders experience extra spins as the seats turn independently. This is what makes the Eejanaika a 4th dimension coaster.

BUILDING BRIEF

Put a new spin on rollercoaster technology, to give riders a whirl of a time.

Designer: S&S Arrow

Key location: Fuji-Q Highland, Yamanashi, Japan

THE NEXT DIMENSION

The Eejanaika circuit only features three upside down turns, known as inversions, but with the added spin of the seats, the riders are turned a tummy-twisting 14 times during the ride. The seats are rotated on a horizontal axis that sticks out perpendicular to the track, and those tracks are the key to the extra spins.

The ride has two sets of tracks that run alongside each other – one set for the cars to run on, the other set to control the seat turns. In certain places the tracks run closer together engaging a simple rack and pinion system that sends the seats spinning.

All in a spin on Eejanaika

LIFT
The car climbs up the lift towards the first terrifying drop.

STATION

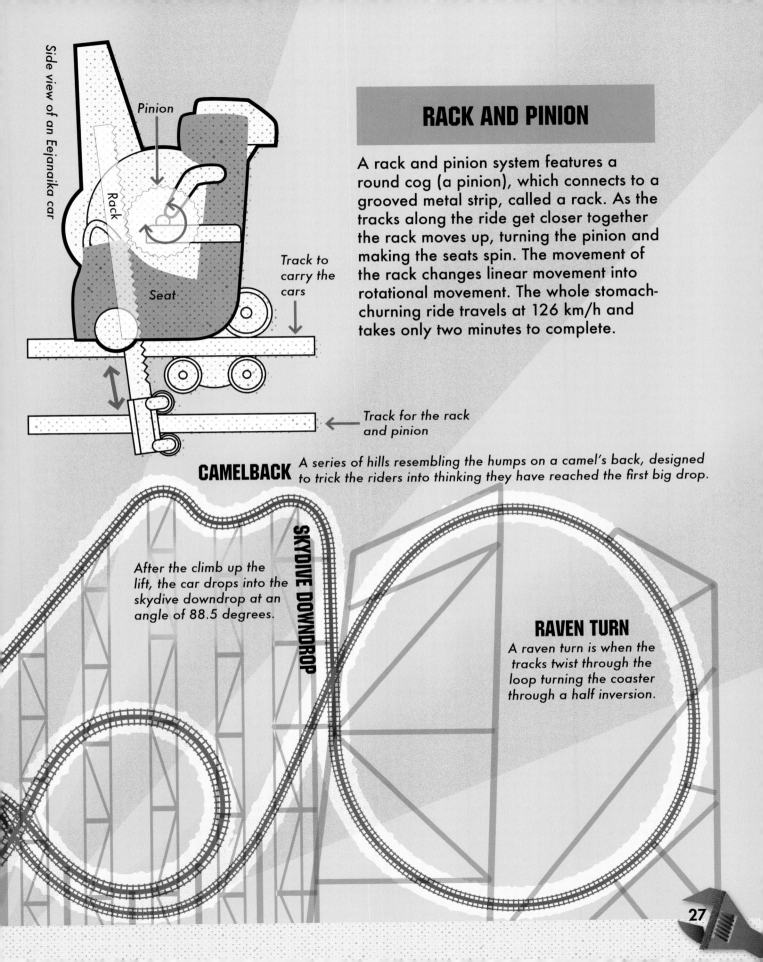

Side view of an Eejanaika car

Pinion

Rack

Seat

Track to carry the cars

Track for the rack and pinion

RACK AND PINION

A rack and pinion system features a round cog (a pinion), which connects to a grooved metal strip, called a rack. As the tracks along the ride get closer together the rack moves up, turning the pinion and making the seats spin. The movement of the rack changes linear movement into rotational movement. The whole stomach-churning ride travels at 126 km/h and takes only two minutes to complete.

CAMELBACK *A series of hills resembling the humps on a camel's back, designed to trick the riders into thinking they have reached the first big drop.*

SKYDIVE DOWNDROP

After the climb up the lift, the car drops into the skydive downdrop at an angle of 88.5 degrees.

RAVEN TURN

A raven turn is when the tracks twist through the loop turning the coaster through a half inversion.

FASCINATING FACTS

Fairground rides are constantly changing with engineers seeking different ways in which the rider or the carriage can move around.

One of the earliest rollercoaster rides was **Les Montagnes Russes à Belleville,** *which appeared in France in 1817. This featured a heart-shaped design, with two cars loading at the top of the track and then racing downhill in opposite directions. Each car gathered enough momentum on the way down to power the cars back up the slope to meet again at the top.*

Shweeb *in New Zealand is a pedal-powered eco ride. Schweeb has one-person pods attached to an overhead rail. Riders climb in, lie down and pedal as fast as they can around the track. The pods can reach speeds of up to 50 kph!*

Skycycle *in Japan is another pedal-powered eco ride that is much slower than Shweeb, but no less scary as twin-pedalled bikes travel along the track high above the ground.*

The first **helter skelter** *was seen at a fair in Hull, UK in 1905. The pull of gravity and a smooth slide transport riders round and down to the bottom.*

LAS VEGAS

The Stratosphere hotel in Las Vegas, USA has four terrifying rides at the top of its 350 m tower.

Thrill seekers bungee jump 261 m from the hotel tower on the **Sky Jump**. —

The **X-Scream** is a rollercoaster that sends riders over the edge of the tower, where the track see-saws to make them think they'll fall to the ground.

On **Insanity**, a gigantic arm extends beyond the edge of the tower, spinning and tilting riders so they can look at the stomach-churning view below.

The **Big Shot** is a drop ride that uses pneumatic motors to send riders up to a height of 329 m above ground level ... and back down to the tower again. —

29

FURTHER INFORMATION

BOOKS

Fairgrounds by Jane Bingham (Wayland, 2015)

Amazing Jobs: Engineering by Colin Hyson (Wayland, 2016)

A History of Britain in 12 Feats of Engineering by Paul Rockett (Franklin Watts, 2015)

WEBSITES

National Fairground Archive:
www.sheffield.ac.uk/nfca/researchandarticles/fairgrounds

Website for Dingles Fairground Heritage Centre in Devon:
www.fairground-heritage.org.uk

Science facts and information on how rollercoasters work:
https://science.howstuffworks.com/engineering/structural/roller-coaster.htm

Design and make a green energy fairground ride with this STEM resource:
www.stem.org.uk/resources/elibrary/resource/31516/green-fairgrounds

Every effort has been made by the Publishers to ensure that these websites are suitable for children, that they are of the highest educational value, and that they contain no inappropriate or offensive material. However, because of the nature of the Internet, it is impossible to guarantee that the contents of these sites will not be altered. We strongly advise that Internet access is supervised by a responsible adult.

GLOSSARY

A-frame *Load-bearing structure in the shape of a capital letter A.*

axle *The rod or shaft going through the centre of a wheel, on which the wheel revolves.*

ballast *Here, crushed stones used to hold the track in place.*

canopy *A cover that provides decoration or shelter.*

circuit *A complete path for an electrical current to pass through.*

conductive/conductor *A material that transmits electricity, heat or noise well.*

cranking rod *A bar connecting and passing movement from a rotating gear to another part of a machine.*

designer *A person who thinks up ideas and draws out plans.*

electrical circuit *The flow of electric power around a circuit.*

electromagnet *A soft metal core made into a magnet by passing electric current through a coil surrounding it.*

engineer *A person who designs and often oversees the construction of a machine or structure.*

force *A push or a pull on an object.*

foundations *The load-bearing parts of a building or structure, often underground.*

friction *Resistance between two surfaces that are moving over each other.*

gear *A wheel with teeth that slots together with others like it. A gear is used to transmit power from one part of a machine to another.*

gravity *A force of attraction between all objects. Earth's gravity makes objects fall to the ground and keeps us from floating off into space.*

horizontal *Parallel to the ground or the horizon.*

hydraulics *A machine controlled or powered by liquids under pressure.*

iconic *Widely recognised, famous, outstanding.*

inertia *This describes how an object will stay moving until it is stopped by an outside force.*

innovative *Advanced, new, inventive.*

kinetic energy *The energy an object has because it is moving.*

laws of motion *The three main laws of physics.*

magnet *Iron or another metal that attracts or repels similar materials.*

magnetic field *The area around a magnet where its forces act.*

mass *Can describe weight, size or number.*

mechanism *The working parts of a machine.*

momentum *An object that is moving has momentum.*

motion *Movement.*

mule *The offspring of a donkey and a horse.*

Newton, Sir Isaac (1642–1727) *One of the most important scientists of all time. He wrote the three laws of motion.*

pendulum *A weight hung from a fixed point so that it can swing freely.*

perpendicular *At an angle of 90 degrees to the ground or another surface.*

piston *A disc or short cylinder that moves inside a closed tube, pushing against a liquid or a gas.*

pneumatic *The energy stored within compressed air.*

potential energy *Energy stored for later use.*

pulley *A wheel with a grooved edge that a rope can run through. It makes lifting heavy objects much easier.*

ratchet *A device made up of a bar or wheel with angled teeth allowing movement in one direction only.*

spectacle *Something amazing or entertaining to watch.*

spring *A device that can be pulled or pressed but always returns to its original shape.*

steel *A strong, hard metal formed from iron, carbon and other materials.*

stress *Here, stress means the forces acting on a structure.*

tension load *A pulling force.*

traction engine *A heavy engine that burns coal to produce steam which is used to power machines or move heavy loads.*

trajectory *The path followed by a moving object.*

winch *A lifting device that turns a chain around a drum or tube.*

INDEX

Franklin Watts

Published in paperback in Great Britain in 2019
by The Watts Publishing Group
Copyright © The Watts Publishing Group, 2017

All rights reserved.

Series editor: Paul Rockett
Series design and illustration: Mark Ruffle
www.rufflebrothers.com
Consultant:
Andrew Woodward BEng (Hons) CEng MICE FCIArb

ISBN 978 1 4451 5528 9

Printed in China

Franklin Watts
An imprint of
Hachette Children's Group
Part of The Watts Publishing Group
Carmelite House
50 Victoria Embankment
London EC4Y 0DZ
An Hachette UK Company
www.hachette.co.uk
www.franklinwatts.co.uk

MIX
Paper from
responsible sources
FSC® C104740
FSC
www.fsc.org

Discarded

FA **ID**

RIDES

SALLY SPRAY
WITH ARTWORK BY MARK RUFFLE

A SPRING TREASURY
of Recipes, Crafts and Wisdom

ANGELA FERRARO-FANNING & ANNELIESDRAWS

HEY, this book was a **REALLY GOOD CHOICE!**

Not just because it's a **GREAT BOOK** (of course we'd say that), but because it is **PRINTED ON RECYCLED PAPER** made from 100% post-consumer waste. Turning a tree into new paper uses a lot of energy, water and chemicals. But turning waste paper into fresh paper again uses a lot less of those resources.

Did you know that most picture books are made in countries on the other side of the world, so they travel a long way to get here? This special book was printed right here in the UK, so the **CARBON FOOTPRINT FROM SHIPPING IS LOWER**, too.

This more **PLANET-FRIENDLY** way of making books costs more, so why did we bother? Because at Ivy Kids we know that our young readers will inherit the world we create today, and we think those children want a **HEALTHY, HAPPY PLANET**. (As well as brilliant books to read).

WE HOPE YOU ENJOY IT!

IVY KIDS

CONTENTS